Your De-Cluttering Book

&

The Art of Letting Go

Also by Margaret Cutler

DeCluttering: the Art of Letting Go

Watch for more at https://www.mangotiger.com.au.

Table of Contents

Dedicated to all my clients who have given me so much trust with their personal lives to let me help them with de-cluttering their subconscious minds to de-clutter their homes and their life.

Margaret Cutler

1

Disclaimer

All the information, exercises, techniques, skills and concepts contained within this publication are of the nature of general comment only and are not in any way recommended as individual advice. The intent is to offer a variety of information to provide a wider range of choices now and in the future, recognizing that we all have widely diverse circumstance and viewpoints. Should any reader choose to make use of the information contained herein, this is their decision and the contributors (and their companies) authors and publishers do not assume any responsibilities whatsoever, under any condition or circumstances. It is recommended that the reader obtain their own independent advice.

FIRST EDITION 2023

Margaret Cutler

This book is dedicated to all my clients and friends who have trusted me with their lives and given me so much insight into the subconscious mind.

My client's stories are all true. Only the names and identifying information has been altered. In some circumstances one or two clients' details have been combined where it does not affect the outcome nor the information.

Testimonials

"The first step in crafting the life you want is to get rid of everything you don't." -Joshua Becker

———————

FOR THOSE OF YOU WHO do not know of my work let me give you something about me before you do the exercises and we begin the work of de-cluttering.

When I was 9 I read a cartoon: an elderly man was sitting in front of his doctor. "Doc," he said, "my left knee really hurts." The doctor, after carefully examining his knee concluded: "There is nothing that I can see that is wrong with your knee, it's because you are 80."

" Well Doc," said the man: "Thank you, but my other knee is 80 too and it doesn't hurt a bit!"

This started me thinking. Why was it one knee that was hurting and not the other? Why was it the left knee and not the right knee? If it was because he was 80 then both knees should be aching and not just one.

Why when a child is hurt does a mother's kiss often stop the pain?

So I started studying the mind and looking at what could possibly create our problems with our health, our work, our relationships and our home. Could there be something other than a purely physical cause?

As a secondary school English teacher I witnessed students with a poor aptitude for study succeed while others failed who should excel. It seemed that if I expected a student to do well they generally did.

When I got rid of cancer a few years ago my doctor said something similar to me "there are some people who should live and don't and there are some people who live despite all the cards being stacked against them."

This really reinforced for me that there is much more to people's lives than we realize and for students far more than just putting in lots of effort. I wanted to know more.

So I have now been working in this field for 43 years successfully helping thousands of people to make significant changes to their lives and overall success; and I found that in a lot of people de-cluttering the house is one of the most important things they could do.

My intention in writing this book is to help you understand how your subconscious mind rules your world and that whatever it thinks it will create no matter what your conscious mind thinks or believes at the time.

Living a cluttered life does not mean you are an extreme hoarder that you often see on the TV; shows where you have to step round things to get into a room or where you can't find anything for the mess.

We all have clutter to a greater or lesser degree. We all keep things that we no longer need or use. In fact the 'third drawer from the top' is famous for housing things that we don't know where else to put them.

I understand that a Finnish proverb goes along the lines of "happiness is a place between having too little and having too much."

You might just be wishing for a stress free environment at home or you might be moving house and need to get rid of everything you don't want to take with you and maybe it's 'stuff 'that won't fit in the new home. Whatever your reason for de-cluttering, this book will help you to get rid of the emotional charge you have that is making you keep things you no longer want

In this book I give you techniques and exercises to help you release any thoughts, beliefs or emotions that are causing you to live a cluttered life where you keep things no matter whether they are things you love or hate or never use. Your home should be a living space and not just a storage space.

These are techniques I have been using for years as I was brought up by a mother who was a minimalist; in other words she had what was necessary and aesthetically pleasing but did not have things that had no use or that she did not love.

There was nothing ever out of place in her home. She used to say that by keeping things to a minimum she could clearly see what she needed, she saved both time and money, and most important of all, she did not have to constantly dust items!!

By reading this book you will also discover:

The underlying inner thoughts, beliefs and emotions that determine your life and the items you are keeping

How to recognize and overcome ingrained *thought patterns* that are influencing you.

How to achieve the quality of life you may have only dreamed about by applying proven, universal laws and by being true to yourself and your values.

That you don't need any tools or equipment to help you de-clutter other than 4 large boxes.

Your Subconscious Mind

Although our conscious mind has the power of reason and can therefore decide the best action, *it is the subconscious mind that determines what our life is going to be like.*

It is called the <u>subconscious </u>mind for one very good reason: its thoughts, beliefs and emotions remain hidden from us until they manifest in some unexpected way, more often than not through an illness or marriage problems or...really anything positive or negative that is happening now.

I don't want you to think our subconscious mind is our enemy, far from it. Our subconscious mind is always protecting us so that even if we are chronic hoarders it is there looking after us.

Behind every problem there is a positive thought or emotion or belief: it is just that while we are trying to overcome our problem it's not always easy to see a positive.

Let me explain a little further.

The subconscious mind cannot judge, nor can it tell the time. Whatever we take into our subconscious mind at any stage of our life will influence us until we recognize these thoughts, beliefs or emotions and set them free. Once we let go of these negatives our mind returns to a core of wellbeing.

The mind always tries to protect us from something.

For instance:

Marika Mulqueen, who was only the second woman in the world to ride the Tour de France stage for stage to the professional schedule (the first was in 1910), rang me to help her get rid of a bad cold the week before she was to ride the Tour de France route. She was extremely worried. She not only had to fly to France, she also had to ride 3500 kilometres in 3 weeks! She could not afford to be ill.

We worked on all her fears of not being able to complete the Tour, her fears of holding the men up, her fears of not being fit enough

(she had not put in any really serious training for this event as it was a last minute decision of hers to enter it).There were a lot of issues she was dealing with including not being able to speak the language in each country she would pass through. So her subconscious mind gave her an 'out.' It gave her a cold. NOW she had a good excuse if she didn't ride well, she was sick.

Fortunately, once she recognized and released these thoughts and emotions, her mind was able to let go of the fears and consequently the need for the cold. While we talked on the phone, she did the releases. She found she was improving dramatically and by the next day she was well. She was able to fly out, completed the 3500 km ride in 3 weeks and made history.

Marika's cold is a classic example of what our minds can do: it will give us a way to avoid something if we need it; and it is exactly the same for the things in our home or when we are keeping things that no longer enhance our lives.

So, the saying that things happen for a reason is true. Once we know the reason behind our problem our mind will let it go comfortably and easily.

You will find that my techniques are very simple to do but have a great impact AND they will change not only your home but also your life!

By doing the exercises you will find many areas of your life will improve. We are meant to be healthy, happy, joyous, successful and abundant. In fact we are meant to have a healthy mind and a healthy body. It is only our resistances or blocks that stop us living an abundant life.

Some of the exercises will only take a couple of seconds, some a couple of minutes and some will take a bit longer. Don't worry, I've written the exercises in such a way that you will find them effective in identifying and then releasing the negative thoughts, beliefs and emotions that you no longer need.

Remember, most people find change threatening so if you find yourself putting off doing the exercises, or you go to do them and they feel difficult, or you feel angry, tired, lethargic, don't be disillusioned: that is just your mind putting up some resistance to change and if you persist you will succeed.

I don't know of anyone who hasn't looked at a pile of 'things' that need clearing out and thought of putting it off until another time. That's why it's good to have a clear vision of what you want your space, desk, room or house to look like once it's decluttered. This vision will keep you motivated to keep going. If you get stuck think of the end result and keep that vision front of mind. Even clearing out just one item is a motivator and will show you that you can do it!

It's also good to start small so you can see the difference it makes and you feel more motivated to keep on going. Just don't try to do it all at once, especially if there is a lot to do as you will probably give up. Just set some time aside to do one thing each week and you will be amazed at how much you get done.

Make decluttering an everyday routine so it doesn't pile up into an intimidating task e.g. Put away things as you finish with them; put used clothes in the laundry or straight into the washing machine; hang the keys on the key hook as you enter your house; take shoes off and put them on to the shoe rack straight away; put jewellery into the jewellery box as you take it off. These are simple things to do but they all help you clean up and then prevent your house becoming cluttered again.

I have deliberately written this book in such a way that even just reading it will activate your subconscious mind to work towards having the space you want.

Then, one day, for no apparent reason at all (!) you will feel compelled to do the exercises and you will then do them comfortably and successfully. (And then you will say "Why didn't I do these before, they are easy to do but Wow, the impact they have! Or words to that effect!)

This book will clearly demonstrate that you are the creator of everything that happens to you; it will reconnect you to your core of well-being and your natural zest for life will return.

This is not some 'think positive and you will receive' type of book. These techniques WORK and have worked for 43 years for people from all cultures, backgrounds and belief systems and I know they will work for you.

By doing these exercises you will:

- Unlock and utilize the power of the subconscious mind
- Clear out unwanted things and people from your life
- Clean up your space
- Free yourself to explore new opportunities
- Start yourself on the path to great health and vitality

This book works well for:

- People who are living in a 'crowded' house
- People who have inherited all their families goods and don't know what to do with them.
- People who feel they cannot throw things out for whatever reason
- People who want to make sure their subconscious mind is making healthy choices
- People who just feel fed up, as if they can't do anything
- People who are worried about their health

De cluttering is about helping you achieve mental, physical, emotional and spiritual freedom.

What you will need before you start:

To succeed you will need:

- An open mind where your only expectation is of change
- To make a special note to re-visit any tasks that make you angry, skeptical or afraid
- To buy a notebook that you really like making sure the size, colour and shape suit you. Do not just grab any old book. Find a book you like and see how it feels. If it feels great, buy it.

If you have no feelings towards it, keep looking. This book must be one that feels really good to you. This simple act of working with a book you love (or anything else in your life) will subtly draw more joy and therefore health and wellbeing into your life.

Possibilities!

De-cluttering will not only change the way you think about your life but it will change the way you see things, the way you do things and the way you interact with other people.

Life altering experiences such as having a baby, changing jobs, moving house or financial worries can cause things to pile up and it becomes harder to be motivated to clean up when there is stuff piling up each day.

People tend to think that they will fix it tomorrow but as we know, tomorrow never comes and the longer it takes to be motivated the less likely they are to start. Approach de-cluttering as an opportunity for personal growth as we are letting go of the past to make space for new experiences and opportunities.

Key Things You Should Know Before You Begin

N o Shame, No Blame

Things 'just are' and we are working through a process to re-connect with your core of wellbeing so you can have the life you want. So stop beating yourself up!

Start small by doing the first release in this book and then the next one. Even if you just do one release a day you will be moving forward. Don't worry about how much there is to do to declutter your house. You may have been living there for 40 years and don't really know what is in every drawer.

Over time things have been put away and forgotten. That doesn't matter. The thing to do is to start and as you work through the exercises you will find that it will become easier and easier for you, in fact you may get to really enjoy the process.

If you are anxious to do something now while reading this book you can start just by moving obvious rubbish out to the bin. If you have wastepaper baskets in various rooms empty them now. This one act will help motivate you.

RATING THE EMOTIONAL IMPACT OF THINGS IN YOUR HOME

Whenever you feel an emotion (resistance) give it a rating out of 10. A rating of 10 means you have the maximum emotional charge to this item while a rating of 0 means there is no emotional charge.

When you want to give something a rating, relax and without conscious thought allow a number to come to mind. That number is the correct rating.

When you are releasing an emotion it is important that you keep doing the exercise I give you until you reach a 0 rating. Only then will you have made the necessary changes in the subconscious mind.

TAPPING EXERCISE

This exercise is based on Thought Field Therapy (TFT) or as it is often called Emotional Field Therapy (EFT) an amazingly easy technique developed by Gary Craig and further developed by Nick Ortner involving tapping on the acupuncture/meridian points to clear emotions/resistance.

It is the quickest and easiest way to release, remove and delete an emotion from the subconscious mind.

If you are already familiar with TFT/EFT you will notice that I don't get you to do the whole sequence for tapping all of the time although you can if you want.

I have found that certain emotions react well to certain points tapped, however everyone is different and you will soon discover what works best for you. I sometimes start by tapping on one point and if I find the rating does not reduce then I will do the whole sequence. Other times just tapping the one point works well.

The tapping sequence:

Karate chop (side of either hand): tap here to set up your tapping session by saying out loud twice " Even though I have all this clutter in my life I accept myself completely and deeply."

Then tap through the following points while making a statement about what it is you want to release. (This is just an overview of the points as I go into more details in the actual exercises):

Top of eyes

Side of eyes

Under eyes

Top lip

Bottom lip

Collarbone

Under arms

Top of head

If you feel tapping isn't for you then simply *feel* the emotion and imagine sending it out to the sun to be destroyed. After you do this a couple of times the mind will know exactly what you want it to do and it will become easier to let the emotion go.

You can also use an imaginary vacuum cleaner to vacuum up the emotions; then throw the vacuum cleaner onto an imaginary moving walkway which takes it straight up to the sun to be burnt up.

LET'S GET STARTED

PHOTOS: PLEASE DO NOT MISS THIS STEP

You will notice that in all of my books I ask you to do this step so you can clearly see the changes that are happening not only to your house but also to you physically. I have seen clients who have heavily lined faces with deep creases on their foreheads lose those creases as they do the exercises, release the identified emotions, thoughts and beliefs and start to clean up their home.

As you do each of the exercises you are not just getting rid of 'stuff', you are releasing the blocks you have in your subconscious mind and so your physical appearance changes for the better.

Whatever you do take a photo of yourself BEFORE you do any of the exercises contained within this book. Make sure you are facing the camera and it is a very clear photo.

Ideally you would have a friend or yourself take the photos TODAY

- A close up photo of you facing the camera
- Left side on
- Right side on
- One of your whole body facing the camera including hair and shoes

Take a photo of every room in your house or your own room if you live with others

- Your room in general
- Inside your cupboards
- Inside your drawers

Take a photo of your office

- Your desk top
- Each drawer in your office

Take a photo of your car both inside and out. Do not wash the car if it needs washing and do not tidy it. Just take the photos as it is now. No one else will see your photos so it doesn't matter what state the home, office or car is in.

Once you have your photos, add today's date and store them away safely because in a very short time if you fully participate in the exercises you will be amazed at the changes you will make.

Because we forget how bad things were once the house is cleaned up and the emotional reaction is over, we need photos to show us the changes.

The best example of this Apex Effect is how quickly women forget labour pains. And if we can forget THOSE pains it is not hard to imagine that we might forget what our home really looked like when we first picked up this book to start reading it.

USING METAPHYSICS OR MANIFESTATION: ASKING FOR WHAT WE WANT

We are born into a world that will supply us with everything we want as long as

1) we ask for it by setting an intention

2) we have no resistance to having it

3) we take action

4) we allow it to manifest.

But how do we go about this asking or setting an intention ?

Imagine what your home would feel like if everything had its own place, there was plenty of space and the air felt fresh and clean.

As you imagine living in this wonderful, free space you know you want it, you feel excited and thrilled to have it. You go about your day thinking about it and imagining yourself having it.

Once you *feel the excitement* of having it, it's as if you have sent a message out to the universe for it to deliver it to you. As absolutely everything is energy, every time you *feel the feeling* of having that space you are giving a clear directive, or setting an intention to have it.

Then you take the necessary actions to enable you to have it and it will be yours.

In 1972 I wrote a bucket list of all the places I wanted to visit. I'd forgotten about it over the years however the other day while cleaning out my membox (a memory box of precious photos and items I treasure) I found my list tucked away inside. Without consciously thinking about this list over the years I now realised that I have travelled to all the places that I had put on my list all those years ago.

I didn't know it at the time but I had followed all 4 steps of manifestation, of getting what I wanted: by writing my list I set the intentions; by putting money aside for travel I was taking action; the order of the countries I visited represented my resistance (I went to the 'easier' places on my own first (no resistance) or with others in a group (some resistance to traveling solo). Every trip on my list has manifested for me. It's time to make another list!!

So let's apply this to your house. If you want a house in which you feel comfortable, safe and easy to live in without clutter use the following metaphysical method:

Step 1: You ask or set your intention for a clean, tidy, welcoming and easy to use house by imagining it and feeling what it is like to live in it. Don't think about what it is like now, only think and feel the emotion of living in the perfect house for you.

Step 2: Make sure there is no subconscious resistance to you having it. (see the steps below to understand and remove this resistance)

Step 3:Take whatever action you need to get it (we will work through this together)

Step 4: Allow it to manifest

SUBCONSCIOUS RESISTENCE

If there is no subconscious resistance in you to stop you having the house you want, then it will be yours.

The longer it takes for your new spacious apartment or home to show up indicates the amount of resistance you have within you. Please be patient with yourself, the fact you have the desire for living in a lovely space means that you are already on the road to having it.

The world is actually giving us what we want already because whatever we think about, we get. Good or bad, whatever state our house is in we have created it by our thinking.

A lot of people think this is terrible because they equate this with blaming themselves. I actually think it is great because it means that if we create something then we can un-create it!

It puts us fairly and squarely in the driver's seat, back in control of our life. It gives us the opportunity to do something positive about it.

THE SUBCONSCIOUS MIND

There are two important things to remember about the subconscious mind:

1. The subconscious mind cannot tell the difference between yesterday, today or tomorrow. It only works in NOW time.

This means that what we believed and took into our subconscious mind as a child is what we believe as an adult *unless we change* that belief or emotion.

That's why so many self-help books suggest healing the child within. In other words, they suggest healing the emotions of the child that are held in the subconscious mind which are influencing our adult choices.

Let's say you were playing in the lounge with a special statue that belonged to your grandmother. For some reason it broke, you feel really worried about it so instead of saying something to her, you hid under the table.

Your subconscious mind will choose to remember something significant from that incident. Let's say it was the awful feelings, of having broken something precious to grandma, along with the feeling of security hiding under the table gave you.

Over the years you forget all about the broken statue however you rarely find the opportunity to visit grandma, normally meeting her on zoom or phoning her.

Then one day as an adult you visit her and your grandma asks you to move an item from her coffee table to the sideboard.

You start to shake and feel as if you want to hide under the table! Yet you are an adult and know this is an extreme reaction to just being asked to move the model from one place to another.

You notice that this reaction (although inexplicable and concerning) is normal for you because any time someone asks you to move anything you start to shake and want to hide. You have actually caught yourself looking for a table to hide under even though you don't follow through with the actions.

This finally brings you to me to find out what is going on. Sometimes I think I should call my business:'The last resort' for the number of times people have said to me: "This is my last resort. I've tried everything there is to try and if this doesn't work I'm giving up."

Throughout your life your subconscious mind remembers how frightened you were years ago at grandma's house when you broke her valuable statue. Your subconscious mind has protected you by making sure you subconsciously avoided visiting your grandmother's house and in fact stopped you moving items in your house and now your house feels cluttered.

This is your subconscious mind protecting you, wanting to get you away from the awful memory of breaking the statue. Unfortunately, as an adult you also find that once you put something on a table or sideboard or anywhere really, that's where it stays!!

Until you deal with the underlying fear of breaking something and wanting to hide, you will continue to avoid moving things. No matter how many times you are asked to clean up the desk, or kitchen or anywhere really, you just can't seem to do it.

1. The subconscious mind cannot judge

As you can see the subconscious mind cannot judge, no matter how old you are. It cannot tell the difference between something that is true and something that is false. It merely reacts to the information that it is given.

The following is a great exercise that you and your partner can do to prove that the subconscious mind will believe absolutely anything.

You will need your partner to work with you so that you can establish the difference between a 'switched on' (yes) and a 'switched off' (no) answer.

- Ask your partner to hold his or her arm straight out from the side, palm down

- Ask your partner if he or she knows any reason why you can't put some pressure on that arm. (Sprained? Sore? Formerly broken? Surgery?) If the answer is yes switch to the other arm

- Ask your partner to say "yes" and then with two fingers placed at the wrist, muscle test by gently pushing on the arm for 2 seconds. You do not have to put a lot of pressure on the arm, slight pressure will still give a result.

- Note whether the arm starts to move downwards, wobbles or remains rigid.

- Now ask your partner to say 'no" and then with two fingers placed at the wrist, muscle test by gently pushing on the arm for 2 seconds.

- Note whether the arm starts to move downwards or wobbles or if it remains rigid

- You now have a difference between the two muscle tests - a rigid test is a 'switched on' or 'yes' answer whilst a wobbly test is a 'switched off' or 'no' answer.

- Now say to your partner: "There is a gate in the back of your neck and the gate is closed so no energy can go through the gate."

- Muscle test with two fingers placed at the wrist, by gently pushing on the arm for 2 seconds.

- Note the result.Now tell the person the gate is open.

- Muscle test with two fingers placed at the wrist, by gently pushing on the arm for 2 seconds.

- Note the result.

IT IS IMPORTANT THAT you make sure that you finish this exercise by telling your partner: 'There is no gate and your energy flows freely.' Test for a 'switched on' or 'yes' result and keep repeating this until you get a switched on response..

Most of the time you will get a wobbly or 'switched off' test for a closed gate and a rigid or 'switched on' test for an open gate. Yet we both know that there is no gate in the person's neck!

This muscle test is a very quick way to show you that our subconscious mind *will believe anything without judgement*, so it is not difficult to imagine that it can take in all sorts of stresses, false beliefs, fears and anxieties as we grow up.

These emotions stay below our level of consciousness in our subconscious mind until something happens to trigger or activate them.

DAILY WRITINGS

While reading The Vein of Gold by Julia Cameron I came across one of the simplest and best morning exercises for clearing the mind and improving life that I have seen and so I am passing it on so that you too can experience its impact.

You will need an A4 writing book and a pen. (Make sure that you get a book that you really like)

Each morning write at least 3 single sided pages of anything that comes to mind. There are no rules as to what to write. No guidelines other than to write. But the best time is first thing in the morning.

Write.

1. At least 3 pages

2. About anything

3. By hand (preferably not on your computer)

That's it. Julia Cameron states that this will "comfort you, console you, empower you, stimulate you, intrigue you, challenge, irritate and activate you."

I would like to add that it would also help you release negative thoughts, beliefs and especially emotions so that you will start to see a shift in your health and wellbeing.

You will be amazed by what you write when you have no planned agenda. Just writing "stuff" gives you an opportunity to whinge, grizzle, whine, celebrate and dream.

By free flowing with your writing you will clear your mind of all the things that annoy, irritate and hurt that are so often expressed though holding on to unwanted items.

If you do this long enough it will clear out the blockages you have and you will certainly create a much healthier mind and a much healthier home.

The key to this is not to think about what you write. Just write whatever comes to mind no matter what it is and how disconnected the thoughts are.

This allows the subconscious mind to 'download'. You will get some pretty good insight into what you are holding onto below the level of consciousness that influences every aspect of your life *without you even knowing it*.

Write by hand and not on the computer. By writing by hand you give yourself time, you write the truth and you gain insight. Speed is not important here. Truth is.

Cameron also suggests that you don't reread what you have written unless it is months later and then only to see if there are any themes showing up.

Oh, and never let a friend read them.

NEW IDEAS, NEW OPPORTUNITIES

Have you recognized that the more cluttered the house is the more cluttered your mind is while you find you are doing less and les exercise and thereby becoming less heathy or strong?

Maybe you have felt ill for so long that you feel you don't have the energy to clean up. The great irony of this is that you won't get the energy unless you do clean up.

There is also a metaphysical reason we need to constantly simplify and get rid of the clutter in our life. Sure, it cleans up the place and it looks better, but of far more importance is that de-cluttering *creates a vacuum* and since nature abhors a vacuum it will rush to fill it straight away but this time with something that you will love and enjoy having. It doesn't always have to be something tangible either, your mind may well fill the space with beautiful music.

When we de-clutter all the things that we no longer need, we free our mind to embrace new ideas, opportunities and people. If you are ill you will be amazed at how much better you will feel and how miraculously you now find the very doctor or therapist or medicine or product that you need to help you get well.

There is more to this exercise than merely throwing out old, unwanted stuff. This exercise is the beginning of us removing subconscious resistance; creating the vacuum and activating the Law of Attraction so we can manifest everything we want.

STARTING THE DECLUTTERING PROCESS

So, let's start to clean up your house or apartment. The smaller your house or apartment ideally the less clutter you should have as there's limited storage or counter space. If it is your own place then you can find some fabulous storage ideas for little houses on the internet. Some of them are great for larger homes too such as turning the steps into storage drawers or using the space under the stairs for storing suit cases or bulky items, hooks for hanging keys or hats or jackets are great too.

First, before you do anything else , get yourself 4 large boxes or bags

Box 1. Is for those things you know you don't want but no one else would want either, so this goes to the rubbish bin.

Box 2. Is for those things that are still in good condition but that you no longer want so this can be sent to a charity.

Box 3. Is for those things that need repair.

Box 4. Is for those things that need laundering.

As your bedroom should be the most comfortable room in the house, start with your bedroom first. Your bedroom allows you a relaxing, life giving and life renewing sleep.

You will be surprised at how much you will throw out as you systematically go through EVERYTHING in your bedroom down to the mattress on the bed, selecting what stays and what goes into one of the boxes.

Don't let this feel overwhelming to you: it is important to start small as this is less confronting, easier to handle and quicker to see results.

You could start with a drawer first.

1. Empty everything in the top drawer onto your bed.

1. Choose the things you love or that you regularly use. Put just these items back in the drawer and put the drawer back in the cupboard.

1. Create a separate drawer for any seasonal gear e.g. cold weather items such as gloves, goggles, beanie for skiing; or a drawer for swimwear, flip flops, swim cap, goggles, sunscreen.

1. Throw out or give away everything that is still left on the bed.

1. Once you have finished with the first drawer you can either do the second drawer now or if you are busy do it tomorrow. Just make sure you set aside the time to do it and make sure that you follow through with it

1. Continue clearing out each drawer until you have cleaned out every drawer in your bedroom.

As to your clothes, an easy way to know whether you have worn something in the last year is to hang all the clothes with the hanger hooked on the rail facing the one way.

When you next wear an article turn the coat hanger the other way. When you get to the end of the season you will clearly know which clothes you need to keep and which ones you can get rid of. You can get rid of all those on coat hangers that are still facing the original way as you haven't worn them.

But there is more to this process than just clearing the cupboard.

WHAT IF I CAN'T THROW IT OUT EVEN THOUGH I DON'T USE IT?

If you recognized that you can't throw something out that you don't wear, then you are keeping it for *an emotional reason* and not because you might wear it.

Let's say you go through your wardrobe and your immediate reaction is to throw something out.Then you find yourself thinking: 'I really should keep this, it cost so much' and so you put it back in the cupboard. Chances are that you will never wear it.

Just because something was expensive doesn't mean you have to keep it. We have all bought clothes that we think we need for a special occasion only to find that we changed our mind at the last minute and decided to wear something that was already in our wardrobe!

It may also be an indication that you have a money issue or blockage in your subconscious mind about money that you need to release.

You need to release this emotional blockage by doing the following exercise:

TAPPING EXERCISE

- Close your eyes
- Find a rating for the emotion you are feeling : 10/10 means you really cannot throw it out while 1-2/10 means there is only a little bit of resistance to throwing it out
- With the fingers of both hands tap the middle of the top of your head
- Repeat this statement "Even though I cannot throw this (name the item) out I accept myself completely and deeply".
- Continue tapping and repeating the above statement until your eyes open of their own accord.

Now see whether you want to keep the article or throw it out or if the rating is still there or has only reduced a little.

If you still want to throw it out but feel you should keep it repeat the above exercise but this time add the following information:

"Even though I cannot throw this (name the item) out because it (was expensive, OR it is too good, OR it might come back into fashion OR I can't fit into it but will, OR I might need it one day) I accept myself completely and deeply"

You might have all these emotions related to this item so work through each one individually until they are all gone. You may have to do this many times as thoughts, feelings and emotions come to your notice e.g.

"Even though I cannot throw this out because it belonged to (Mum, Dad, favourite relative, friend) I accept myself deeply and completely."

"Even though I feel guilty throwing this out I accept myself completely and deeply"

Do not skimp on this exercise as it is more important than it looks at first glance.

In these exercises you are not just cleaning out your cupboard you are clearing out the negative emotions that are your subconscious resistance to you having everything you wish for including your perfect home and even your health.

If, after doing all these exercises on the one article, you are still uncomfortable throwing it out, put it back in the cupboard and keep doing the exercises I give you throughout this book to clear it of its emotional charge.

Just remember that just for this moment you will put it back into your cupboard with the hanger facing the right way, knowing it is *safe* there. Fundamentally every emotion is hiding a safety issue.

You don't feel worried about throwing out a friend's gift just because it will offend the friend; you resist because you are afraid that if you offend your friend then they won't be friends with you anymore and you will feel lonely or alone and that is a safety issue for you.

Realising this, you can put it back where it is safe (so you are safe!) while you continue to release the thoughts, beliefs and emotions that arose in you. It can take a few days to get rid of these so be patient and just know that you are clearing them out to have the life you want. Once done, you can then move along to the next item.

Once you have gone through your bedroom do not start on another room until you have done the following:

- Take Box 1 to the garbage bin immediately
- Drive to the charity bin to drop off Box 2 immediately
- Mend those items in Box 3
- Launder those items in Box 4

If you cannot drive, either get a friend to deliver these things for you or you can call one of the charities to pick them up. Here in Australia, and I assume it is the same worldwide, there are charities and businesses that will pick up household goods and even rubbish and dispose of those for you for a fee.

Most charities will not take mattresses or bedroom pillows so this paid service is great for getting rid of those. There are also specialised toxic waste and paint waste dumps. Grocery stores such as Woolworths and Coles also have boxes for old phones while Rotary and Apex often have donation days for old eye glasses.

Yu might prefer to sell your items through any of the online markets too as this is a great way to get them out of your house and your life.

Once you have finished that room and thrown out the boxes, laundered and mended the clothes then you can then move on to the next room in the house and so on.

Do not hurry. This is not a speed competition. Your life is worth taking the time and making the effort to do it properly.

BOOKS

Books can be a challenge especially if you love reading as much as I do. If you know you won't read a particular book again you can donate it to the library or to Rotary book sales or any other organisation that will take books. There are still some second-hand book stores which will buy old books as well.

The key is to donate straight away before you have time to think over and perhaps put the book back. If you do put it back, look for the emotional reason for keeping the book. You might be surprised at what you hear your mind say.

Once you have read a book it is highly doubtful that you will read it again. That said, I do not throw out a book that is a great reference book, is one I absolutely love or that brings great memories of when I bought it or was given it. Those are the only ones I will keep.

By donating the books I feel that someone else has the opportunity to get the same pleasure I had when I first read them. It also means that my house is not cluttered and dusty with books that I will never read again.

I have also been known to leave a book in a bus shelter, at the airport or anywhere people are waiting. Although this backfired on me once when I was reading the last pages of a really good book at the airport. I got up to put some rubbish in the bin just a few feet away from me. I put the open book down for about 20 seconds and when I turned round it was gone! I now had to either buy another copy of the almost finished book or wait til I got to a library so that I could read the last pages. (I bought a different book for the trip and went to the library at my destination).

Also do not underestimate the power of this exercise, it will make an incredible difference to you. Just listen to your first, immediate response when you pick up a book or an item. The response will tell you whether the article enhances your life (it immediately feels right to keep it) or if it has a hidden resistance attached to it. (You feel you *should* keep it).

If you have never done this before this exercise can take you a few months to complete, especially as you apply it to every drawer in every room of your home, your office, your car, even to checking your relationships with your friends and family.

This de-cluttering exercise is important and is usually repeated a few times during the year. I like to do it the first week of each month and am always surprised at finding things to throw out. Don't worry, it not only gets easier to do each time you do it but you may surprise yourself by actually looking forward to it.

IF YOUR HOUSE COULD SPEAK, WHAT WOULD IT SAY?

Now have a look at what your house is saying to you. Is there a place of your own within it? Is every room a shared room? Who controls the decorating and style of furniture and its positioning?

As you think about your house think about what it represents to you and see if it also indicates an underlying difficulty that has not been addressed between you, your partner or your family especially if there are one or two members of the family who happily live in a mess while you like open space and everything in its place.

The only way to handle this is to have an open conversation where you state your needs for the shared spaces to be kept tidy while you all can have your own rooms as you like them.

This is important when you have little children too. They love to help clean up their toys and put them away before bed especially if the idea is presented as creating a wonderful space for them to enjoy when they get up tomorrow.

If they are brought up knowing that they must respect the shared spaces by keeping them clean and tidy then you won't have issues with them as they get older and buy their own gear.

Be very careful if you don't like the mess in your children's room. You also have to respect that this is their personal space, just as they have to respect your bedroom.

You can set some rules though such as no food or drinks in the room ; school bags to be emptied and cleaned on the first day of the school holidays (otherwise don't be surprised if you find maggots and rotting food in their bags when they go to pack the night before school starts!)

My young son used to have a very untidy room so one day I thought I would clean it up for him. When he came home from school I proudly showed him what I had done. For about half a second he said it looked great; then he looked worried and finally said: "now I just walk from the door to the bed and that's nothing. Before you cleaned it up I had to climb over the rocks, swim the crocodile infested river, climb the highest mountain and that was much more fun!!

I should have known then that he would turn out to be a very successful and creative man! Oh yes, I never cleaned up his room again although we did have the no food rule.

Don't forget that to de-clutter your house you are also de-cluttering old emotions, thoughts and feelings that are no longer appropriate to who you are now.

Don't feel badly if you recognize that a relationship is no longer a joyous one for you. You may find that your anger, frustration or disappointment with this person is the very thing that is being expressed by the clutter in your garage, shed, spare room or even the whole house.

I had one client who was deeply distressed: her husband George kept his motorbike and tools in the lounge room. He said the bike was important to him and there was nowhere else he could keep it; he felt it didn't matter as they didn't have many visitors nor use the lounge room themselves.

Marcie did not feel she could argue with him: it was his house, she had moved into it after they married and the bike was already there. We did a lot of work on her self-worth and respect for herself before she was able to discuss moving the bike with her husband.

Sandy kept telling me she wanted to move out of a unit and into a house but her partner wasn't interested. He liked living in the city and did not want to move to the suburbs where he would have to commute to work. He meanwhile was complaining about all the mess and that each day she brought home more and more things.

Not only that but her mother kept donating things she thought her daughter would need to help her 'set up house'. They formed a very strong passive -aggressive pact between them to force the issue of moving.

She stored empty boxes under the bed, on top of the cupboards, in the wardrobe. She was sabotaging the unit by making sure it so cluttered that her partner would have to agree to move. Finally the couple split up for many reasons including the fact the unit was so full of stuff and rubbish that finally he could not stand living with it all.

You may find that you have a constant need to change things around, to move the lounge room furniture every few weeks. This may also be a mask or a way of covering up a dissatisfying relationship.

RELATIONSHIPS THAT NO LONGER ENHANCE YOUR LIFE

According to Marianne Williamson

'A relationship is more of an assignment than a choice. We can walk away from the assignment but we cannot walk away from the lessons it presents. We stay with a relationship until a lesson is learned or we simply learn it another way'.

Maybe the concern is as simple as the fact that you are an adult and still living at home with your parents and following their rules rather than developing your own home. You feel that they do not understand your need for your own space so as with Sandy instead of addressing the issue you passively aggressively fill your room so that they will finally realise you need to move out into somewhere of your own.

It would be far better to speak with your parents about your needs; however if you can't do that then there is a subconscious issue that you need to address.

It may be that your subconscious mind believes that you have to stay with your parents to keep them safe (if you suffered from school phobia as a child this will often be the cause of it as children think they are in control of everything around them).

In terms of more adult relationships once something or someone has completed his or her relationship with you it is time to let it go. This way someone else can benefit.

People come into your life for a reason, a season or a lifetime. When you know which one it is, you will know what to do for that person.

When someone is in your life for a REASON, it is usually to meet a need you have expressed. They have come to assist you through a difficulty, to provide you with guidance and support, to aid you physically, emotionally or spiritually.

They may seem like a godsend and they are. They are there for the reason you need them to be. Then, without any wrongdoing on your part or at an inconvenient time, this person will say or do something to bring the relationship to an end.

Sometimes they die. Sometimes they walk away. Sometimes they act up and force you to take a stand.

What we must realize is that our need has been met, our desire fulfilled, their work is done and now it is time to move on'.

EXERCISE 1

Here is one technique for letting go of old relationships:

- Think of a relationship that no longer enhances your life
- Imagine you are face to face with that person
- Thank that person for the relationship you have had
- Release that person to their highest good

EXERCISE 2

Here is another technique for letting go of relationships that have hurt you in the past:

- You are sitting in a chair
- Imagine the person is sitting in a chair opposite you
- Say to that person: " I get so angry when you ...." (fill in the sentence with as much detail as you can)
- Then say to that person: " When I think of what our relationship could have been I resent it when you..." (fill in the sentence with as much detail as you can)"
- Now imagine a light shining through your heart to the other person's heart and quietly allow that light to heal both of you

- Imagine that the person is also forgiving you.

Do this with every person with whom you have had a difficult relationship whether it is now or in the past.

EXERCISE 3

Once you think you have completely forgiven everyone you need to, wait a few days and then ask yourself: "Is there anyone who I need to release or forgive?" Your mind will let you know if there is someone, then you can tap the emotion out or do one or both of the exercises above. .

If you repeat the question at least once or twice a week then by the end of the month you will have released or forgiven everyone you need to.

YOUR POSSESSIONS, YOUR VALUES AND YOUR IDENTITY

You might like to use the following exercise to understand more deeply how your home and what you have in it represents what you value and how that is impacting your health and wellbeing.

Really look at everything you have in your home. Since every object, ornament or piece of art expresses our real selves, looking closely at what we are expressing can give valuable insight into our true identity.

The things you have around you must represent your true values otherwise you will find a way to express that discord.

For example, do all the paintings represent the outdoors, trees, shells, plants, the sea and flowers showing that you really value nature? Are there people in the paintings or is there only one person? What are they doing? What is the emotion they are conveying to you?

Does it feel impossible to get outside as there is so much to do inside that you don't get out in the sun enough? Do you lack Vitamin D?

Listen to what you say as this will give you a clue as to what you value e.g. Do you say that you feel 'cooped up' inside? If so, make time to get outside, it will not only refresh you, give you sunshine and Vitamin D, it will also make you look at your house in a different way and it will help you to throw out the old to bring in the new.

To understand what might be your primary values have a look around your house. *Are there lots of photos of family and friends?* Then family might be an important value. Do you see them often enough?

What about your cookbooks and the vegetable garden? Do they represent your need for healthy eating and living? Is your subconscious trying to tell you to eat better, more organic and fresh food?

As you walk through your home look at every item in relation to its attunement with your identity.

This following exercise also helps with de-cluttering because things that don't match your intrinsic values will stand out thus allowing you to move them out of your home and life.

SIMPLIFY

This is de-cluttering in disguise!

Look for clutter in the following areas:

Social events; Lunches; Parties; Friends dropping in.

Let your friends know the times you will be free for them to drop in and be clear that any other time you will be busy and unable to see them even if you really wanted to.

Are you filling your days with so many social events that you don't have time to do the important things? If so, sit quietly and ask yourself what you are avoiding doing? What are you fearful of? What are you afraid of? How do these social events help you to avoid something and what is that something?

TV, Free to Air, Netflix, Disney

How many paid channels do you have? Do you really need them all? Are they filling your day so you are not lonely? Procrastinating? Afraid of a deadline? Afraid you can't do it? Afraid of failure? Afraid of success? Feel that you have paid for them so must justify the payment?

Toys.

Have your children help you to clean up and clear out. After all the toys are theirs and you don't know the emotional attachment they might have to something you think should be thrown out. If you work with your children you will find that kids are really good at clearing out old toys and are often more ruthless than we adults are.

If they feel that they are contributing to the family (children love to feel important and helpful) then they will be more willing to help clear up the mess they make so that the new day starts fresh and clean.

Busy days.

Do you use your calendar or diary to keep track of your time off? At the beginning of the week fill in time for the things you must do and cross out the time you don't want to be working. Having 'me time' is very important for your mental health and well being.

If you find you can't schedule in 'me time" have a look at the reasons why you can't. Are you afraid of getting into trouble because you have been trained as a child to believe that any time you are not working you are being lazy?

If so, imagine yourself as a young child sitting in front of you the adult. Speak kindly and clearly to your child reassuring him or her that it is absolutely necessary for them to have 'me time'; in fact you want them to have it and you will help them to have it by putting the time out into a diary for them.

Keep chatting to your inner child until they agree with you to have this time out. You will be surprised how this chat will help you the adult to schedule in free time for yourself.

Disorganized days and your 'To do' list

Your calendar and diary are here to keep you on track, along with building a 'to do' list.

'To do' list .

The trick to this list is to put the things you must do first on the list, then the next most important thing to do and so on. Once you have the list competed start to work on the first item only concentrating on that one thing at a time. When you have finished the first item do the next item on the list, only moving to the next one once you have finished this one.

Anything that is left over goes onto tomorrow's list. Now you prioritise this new list.

If you find there are one or more items that keep getting put onto the next day's list, really look at them and see if they are worth doing or if they were just a 'passing thought' and are not really important enough to do.

If this is the case don't put them on tomorrow's list at all. You can get rid of them altogether.

If you feel they will be useful to do 'someday' put them on a separate 'someday' list where they will be safe and you can refer to them should you ever want to.

UNCLEAR THINKING and the WORRY JAR

This generally comes from having too many thoughts going round in your head. To help clear this up first write each thought down on a small separate piece of paper.

Decide if it should go on the 'to do list' or if it is a worry. If it is for the 'to do' list , write it there.

If it is a worry create a 'worry jar'. This is a large clear bottle. You must be able to see anything that is in it.

1. Write down your worry on a piece of paper if you haven't already done so and put the paper in the bottle.

1. Set aside time at the end of the day or end of the week as your worry time.

1. At that time take all the worries out of the bottle and read through

each one.

1. Throw out those that did not come true.

1. Set a timer and really worry about one of the items you have written down.

1. At the end of the time if it needs more worry time put it back in the jar.

1. Choose the next worry and worry over it.

1. At the end of the time if it needs more worry time put it back in the jar.

1. Do this with each worry you have put in the jar.

Over time you will find your head will become clearer and clearer and there will be only be a couple of worries in the bottle to worry about, if any!

SHOPPING

Do you go shopping then have to go to the corner store for forgotten items? Make a list before you go shopping or better still keep a pad and pencil on the kitchen bench or fridge or near the door.

As you use up an item put it on the list. Now when you go shopping you know exactly what you need to buy.

You can also buy two of the same item so you always have a spare; when you start to use the spare one you put it on the list. This way you will never run out.

TELEPHONE CALLS and TEXT MESSAGES

You do not have to answer every call nor reply to every message as soon as you receive them. Although we have gotten used to' instant actions' you are in charge of your life and your life is too important to be responding to all calls just because someone else wants to speak with you.

Voicemail is a godsend for busy people because you can click the button to send their message to voicemail and you can ring them back when you are free.

EMAILS

Some people like to set aside a specific time for answering emails. And they are happily able to ignore the email until that specific time. I like to read, answer or action an email as soon as I receive it. That way it satisfies my curiosity and also gets the work done immediately.

I enjoy receiving emails and don't find that they interrupt my work. Others find them a nuisance. Work out a system that works for you.

To keep the email trail and to enable you to find files easily create folders for each project and put emails you have replied to along with your replies into those folders.

You may like to have the following system but it is entirely your work so do what works for you best.

Project name

Separate file for each project subdivision

Separate file for each person involved in that subdivision or project

It them becomes very easy to see who has emailed you and what your reply has been

YOUR PURSE OR WALLET

I am always amazed by how much people carry in their purse or wallet. Decluttering this is the same as decluttering a drawer.

   a. Tip all the contents out onto a table or bed.
   b. Throw out anything that is out of date (except lottery tickets as you

       might have won! So set aside time to get them checked)

c. Throw out expired coupons and vouchers. Put receipts aside to add to your tax.

d. Throw out any pens that don't work and only keep one pen.

e. Throw out old tissues or scraps of paper or old sweets.

In other words only keep what you need and what you will use that day.

MOBILE PHONES

Mobile phones are seductive and tempting time wasters. We're often too busy scrolling social media feeds to be truly present and engaged in what's happening around and in front of us.

Remove all apps that you don't use, don't need or don't find value in.

DELETED ITEMS ON COMPUTER

What about your deleted items on the computer? You could set yourself the first thing every Monday or every first day of the month to delete the items in the bin, empty cache and restart your computer. It will soon become a habit.

LET'S START TO SPRING clean your whole life. Let's get rid of the past and live now, after all yesterday is over and tomorrow hasn't come yet.

There are two things that have a profound impact on your life: not drinking enough clean water and living in clutter: both of which will 'weigh ' you down both literally and metaphorically.

Lack of water will make you feel hungry when you are in fact thirsty so you will eat when you don't need the food thereby putting on excess weight.

Since the body is made up of 76% or more of water it constantly needs water to keep it healthy. Water cleans both externally and internally, helps eliminate toxins and flushes out your system. Make sure that the water is filtered and chemical free.

Clutter weighs heavily on your mind, prevents you thinking clearly and prevents you taking action; and the dust that accumulates when you have too much stuff can give you asthma and other respiratory diseases.

You know there is clutter (even if it is not obvious because it is hidden behind cupboard doors) when you are upset, when you find yourself saying: "Everywhere I look there are things", "There is so much to do", "I'm overwhelmed". Any of these statements indicate clutter in your life.

They are also a good indication that if you don't do something about them then your subconscious mind will make sure you do.

I have had clients with Chronic Fatigue who could not throw anything out. They were overwhelmed by the things they had and so rather than deal with all the 'stuff' they closed their body down into tiredness which effectively prevented them having to think about throwing anything out!

We had to work on their hidden agenda of fear that was making them keep all their goods. Then very slowly they were able to clean out the house and get back to a more active life.

There is always a positive behind any negative or illness. The mind is always protecting us and sometimes it gives us an illness as a form of protection.

In the above case, my clients had such an emotional charge on throwing out and de-cluttering that it was easier for them to have chronic fatigue because it stopped them having to deal with the clutter and the emotions related to their things.

Now not everyone who has a lot of things is going to get chronic fatigue; however, when there is an emotional charge, a negative belief or a thought that prevents us doing something we really want to do then the mind will give us an excuse or a physical way to prevent us doing that very thing.

We now have created a perfect excuse: 'I would love to clean up this mess/get rid of all this stuff/ but I have chronic fatigue and get so tired all the time that I just can't do it"

Rhonda was a very intelligent, mature scientist whose outstanding work was recognized throughout her profession, however her house was so cluttered she felt that from the moment she walked through her front door she could not function.

As she was a friend and probably because she knew I like everything in its right place without being neurotic about it she asked me to help her sort out the mess. My husband and I spent a couple of days with her, sorting out 50 years of crockery and materials and dresses, years of accumulated things that were never used.

After we cleared it all out she was thrilled, for about 10 minutes. Then her face changed as she exclaimed' Oh dear, now I will be lonely!"

She had lived alone for many years and had not realized that the things she bought and hoarded were replacing real friendships. It also gave me some valuable insight into why some people hoard things.

Another friend of mine, Michael has so much 'stuff' that the house is full, the double garage is full and the attic is full! My thought is that he and his wife each have an underlying fear of not being worthy enough so that they accumulate to prove their worth!

After all, the things collected are valuable so they must have had money to be able to buy them in the first place and must have money now in having a big house to be able to store them.

It is interesting to note that Michael and Anne avoid de-cluttering as much as they can by 'having to' do other things, even though the house is sold and they must move. They even contracted a long settlement so that they had time to go through everything and keep what they valued.

What they are finding is that they have not looked at the stuff they had bought for so long that a lot of it is now rubbish. It is also giving great insight into their need to collect. Anne is developing eye trouble so she can't see what has to be cleared out and Michael is constantly getting sick or feeling 'off' so he does not have the energy to clear it all out.

Whilst helping them to clear out their goods I would also love to work with them to help them clear out the subconscious need for things but I also think it would be very difficult to work with friends, after all this work gets to your deepest fears and friends would probably not want me to know. Still it would be great to see the difference it would make.

There is a danger however that if each of them let go of the feeling of being unworthy they may find that they no longer need the other partner. Perhaps a small or maybe a significant part of their relationship is based on them having the same fear in the subconscious mind so that 'like attracts like."

If you are having trouble throwing out, cleaning up or de-cluttering look at the following list to see if any of it holds an emotional charge for you.

Do you think: 'I can't throw that out because I am dependent...

- On my parents approval of what I have in my house
- On the economy to get a good, better job so I can replace it with something I like
- On a good job for survival (so can't afford...)
- On Unemployment Benefits (so can't afford...)
- On Age Pension (so can't afford...)
- On Medicare/ Medical benefits (so can't afford...)

Whatever you do, do not be annoyed for any emotion that you feel when you are doing these exercises.

What I really would like is for you to understand yourself and know what motivates you to do things. Knowledge is power.

You do not have to throw anything out that you do not want to throw out however if you work towards letting go of the emotional resistance to your 'things' over time you will automatically start to remove those things you no longer need or even like without even realizing it.

GETTING TO THE ROOT CAUSE

You might like to apply the following technique, filling in the gaps as you work through the following questions. It normally takes 5 questions to get to the root cause of any problem however it is OK to keep asking. When you answer these questions, you may get something like this:

If I throw this item out or clean up what will happen to me?

I might need it

If that happens, what will happen?

I will feel wasteful

If that happens, what will happen?

Mum will be angry with me

If that happens, what will happen?

I will feel as if I am choking

———————

IF THAT HAPPENS, WHAT will happen?

I will feel as if Mum will be so angry with me she won't help me

———————

IF THAT HAPPENS WHAT will happen?

I will die.

How old are you?

3 years old

Ultimately at the bottom of most of these problems is a survival fear. For example the person who has so much 'stuff' yet compulsively buys more, may well be covering up loneliness as with Rhonda or a sense of not being worthy as with Michael and Anne.

If I throw this item out or clean up what will happen to me?

I might need it

If that happens what will happen?

I will feel wasteful

If that happens what will happen?

The place will be empty

If that happens what will happen?

I'll have no- one to talk to

If that happens what will happen?

I'll be alone

If that happens what will happen?

I'll be lonely

If that happens what will happen?

I'll be afraid

If that happens what will happen?

I won't know what to do to look after myself

If that happens what will happen?

I might die

How old are you?

4 years old

Once you have gained insight into your subconscious mind you can take each answer and tap it out so that you remove the resistance.

For the example I have given you above, use the tapping sequence as a form of release. When you do your tapping exercise just substitute your own answers for the ones I have given.

TAPPING EXERCISE 1

- Close eyes
- Using fingers of both hands tap the middle of the top of your head
- While tapping repeat this statement until your eyes open "Even though I might need this (name the item) I accept myself completely and deeply"

TAPPING EXERCISE 2

- Close eyes
- Using fingers of both hands tap the middle of the top of your head
- While tapping repeat this statement until your eyes open: "Even though I will feel (wasteful) I accept myself completely and deeply".

TAPPING EXERCISE 3

- Close eyes
- Using fingers of both hands tap the middle of the top of your head
- While tapping repeat this statement until your eyes open: "Even though the place will feel (empty) I accept myself completely and deeply".

TAPPING EXERCISE 4

- Close eyes
- Using fingers of both hands tap the middle of the top of your head
- While tapping repeat this statement until your eyes open: "Even though I'll have (no-one to talk to) I accept myself completely and deeply".

TAPPING EXERCISE 5

- Close eyes
- Using fingers of both hands tap the middle of the top of your head
- While tapping repeat this statement until your eyes open: "Even though (I'll be alone, I'm alone) I accept myself completely and deeply".

TAPPING EXERCISE 6

- Close eyes
- Using fingers of both hands tap the middle of the top of your head
- While tapping repeat this statement until your eyes open: "Even though I'm (afraid) I accept myself completely and deeply".

TAPPING EXERCISE 7

- Close eyes
- Using fingers of both hands tap the middle of the top of your head
- While tapping repeat this statement until your eyes open: "Even though I won't know what to do to (look after myself) I accept myself completely and deeply".

TAPPING EXERCISE 8

- Close eyes
- Using fingers of both hands tap the middle of the top of your head
- While tapping repeat this statement until your eyes open: "Even though I might die I accept myself completely and deeply".

TAPPING EXERCISE 9

- Close eyes
- Using fingers of both hands tap the middle of the top of your head
- While tapping repeat this statement until your eyes open: "Even

though I'm (4) years old I accept myself completely and deeply".

FRIENDS

You may be surprised that I have included friends in this de-cluttering process. There are some friends who are toxic to you; you feel it whenever you are with them as they really drain your energy, annoy you or frustrate you.

Some friends even make you ill!

If you recognize there are people in your life who have a draining effect on you or you feel a change in your body such as a restriction in the throat, a tightening of the diaphragm then it is time to gently release them from your life too. You don't even have to say anything to them about releasing them.

By repeating at least 10 x per day (to activate the Law of Attraction) 'I now have wonderful friends who enhance my life;' your energy shifts and the people who no longer match your vibration move easily and freely away. You will feel free, healthier and so much better.

When you have done this exercise to de-clutter diligently, you will be amazed how free you will feel as you start to bring new positive experiences to yourself without conscious effort.

Imagine what your life will look like in a few short months!!

"There is only one success, to be able to spend your life in your own way" Christopher Morley

While you are de-cluttering did you think of checking out the spare shed where you have things stored that are too good to throw out so you are keeping them for your children? Will they really want them? Are they 'sick at the thought' of having to take Mum and Dad's stuff?

What about gifts received? Just because a friend or relative gave us a gift does not mean we have to keep it. Thank the person when they give it to you because you are thanking them for their gift of love and friendship. If you want the gift, keep it; if not give it to someone else who loves it.

What about family 'stuff' inherited that was too good to throw out but that you really did not want nor need. Would someone else benefit from them? This can be a tricky one. Often we feel guilty if we throw out things we have inherited. Yet it is important to recognise that the items belonged to the relative and not to us. Only if we really love the item should we then keep it.

Sometimes we feel that to throw out the items means we are throwing out the person and nothing could be further from the truth. The item is not the person; we will always have our memories and keeping an item which we don't like, need or want is not what our relative would want for us.

Remember this when you think of leaving your things to your children. Will they really want it? Will they want to clean out your house after you die?

What about the jar/drawer where you toss all the spare pens/pencils/coins? You only need one pen or pencil that you use and a spare so you can throw the rest out. As for the coins, they could be earning some interest in your bank account.

Simone is an amazing person. Happy and successful, she has really mastered the art of being in the here and now. Every time she moves house she has an enormous garage sale and sells everything right down to the last teaspoon!

Then she has great fun buying for her new house so that it always reflects who she is NOW and not where she was 5, 10 or 15 years before.

And do you know she has absolutely brilliant health and fitness. Her life is always evolving and exciting, she never has time nor the need to be sick!

Now I am not advocating that we all do this as it is incredibly expensive to throw everything out and replace it but it has been and still is, fascinating to see how her life evolves and to visit her home knowing that it will represent another aspect of her personality.

Remember I said at the beginning of this book that my mother was a minimalist? One of the tricks I learnt from her was to always have a charity box ready so that anything I realised I no longer needed went straight into that box; then when it was full I would drop it off at the opportunity shop. I also like to start the new year with a fresh house so I have made the habit of every January going through every room, cupboard and drawer in my house and throwing out what I no longer use, need, want nor love.

Then in the first week of every month I work at throwing out 19 items. I don't always get to throw out 19 items but the very fact of starting to clean out unwanted, unused items means that every month I have an opportunity to refresh my life and home.

I am always surprised at how many things I no longer need nor use nor even like.

It is fascinating to see that when I change my home address so I find that there are a lot of items that I loved before that I no longer want. It is as if the new house has a major influence on me and forces me to throw out what no longer suits me. After all, I moved house so something in my psyche has changed otherwise I would still be in the same house with the same items of furniture, clothes and so on.

NUMEROLOGY and YOUR HOME

So let's look at numerology and see if you can see what has changed in your life when you changed houses (and what you no longer need nor want)

Although I use the following system to check the house numbers there are many other systems about. Use whichever one you find most helpful as no one system is perfect for everyone.

Although I can get a fair indication of what aspect of my life I am working on while living in a particular house I normally don't find out the full significance of that number until after I have finally left it.

I also notice the table number when I go to a restaurant. It is interesting to see how many times the number I am randomly given represents exactly what I am working on that day!

If your house number consists of just one digit, that's easy, just refer to the numbers and their meanings given below.

Where the number consists of several digits add them together to get the single number you need. For example:

61 become 7

391 becomes 13 which becomes 4

23 becomes 5

Do not add 11 or 22. They always remain 11 and 22 and are very powerful numbers.

So here are the numbers as I use them. I hope you find them fun, interesting and very enlightening.

Don't worry if you can't get the full picture as yet after all, while you are living in the house you are also still working through its message.

1. New beginnings, sense of self
2. Relationship, joy and happiness
3. Sense of your own will
4. Karma or underground water (often a 4 house will have problems with plumbing or washing machines that overflow, or a leaking swimming pool) The Chinese associate 4 with death
5. Change leading to balance and harmony; being busy
6. Destiny
7. Spiritual completion
8. As above, so below
9. Physical completion; someone living in this house needs to learn unconditional love
10. Converts to 1 however means time between the new beginning or finding of oneself before the next action will take place

11 & 22: These are power numbers and represent that you are 'in flow' with the universe, being the right place at the right time.

I also like to look at the order of the numbers to get more meaning/symbols.

For example when looking at a house number 27, I break the numbers down in the following way:

Number 2 represents joy and is followed by number 7, which represents spiritual completion.

By adding 2 and 7 together we get 9 which symbolizes unconditional love and physical completion

So I would interpret this house as follows: initial joy (2) leads to spiritual completion (7) through learning unconditional love (9).

Once this has been achieved then the people would physically complete with the house (9). In other words they would move on to another house or even pass over.

Many people towards the end of their life move into a house or room whose numbers are or add up to 9, which means physical completion. It also means learning unconditional love; so don't start to worry about dying if you are living in a 9 house!

Janet lives in a number 1 house representing a house of 'new beginnings, sense of self'. She is, to all appearances, an extrovert yet once you know her she is a very dependent personality who is always changing partners and starting jobs ('new beginnings' and 'sense of self')

Perhaps Janet's house is really trying to get her in touch with her own inner core of wellbeing, her 'sense of self' so that she is not so dependent on others and then she might settle.

I also look for any moderating influences such as "a" or "b", the symbolism is still the same; it is just modified in some way.

So an apartment number 2 with a street address of 2a would mean starting with 'joy and happiness' (2) leading to long term modified joy and happiness (2a) or it could mean that one person is happy to stay there (2) while a second person comes and goes (2a).

It's also interesting to watch the changes that take place in people and their health/relationships/career/interests when the Council changes the numbering of their houses!

Now let's apply this numerology to where you live:

1. What is your house number?
2. What is your house number after adding all the digits together? (Do not add 11 to make 2 nor 22 together to make 4).
3. Using the system above what does your number symbolize?
4. What has happened (in detail) to each person's health since living there?
5. Why do you think that you were guided to that house? What has the house taught you or what have you learned since living there?
6. The question then remains: 'Did the person choose the house or did the house choose them?' What do you think?

HOUSE EXERCISE TO GIVE YOU INSIGHT INTO YOUR LIFE

This is a great exercise you can do to gain insight into the energy of your house and how it may be affecting you.

Take an A3 piece of paper and using any colours that appeal to you, draw your house or where you are living now. It makes no difference whether it is your own home or you rent.

Now choose one particular colour that you like:

- Colour in the areas of the house that you feel belong or resonate with you
- Choose another colour and colour in the areas that you feel belong to someone else
- Choose a third colour and colour in the areas that are everyone's shared spaces.

Now speak to your house:

- Tell your house exactly what you think
- Tell your house exactly how you feel about it (without censorship).
- Tell your house if it reminds you of any other house you have lived in
- Tell your house if there is something you particularly like or dislike about it.
- Tell your house how you *feel* when you come home of an evening.

Now ask the house to converse with you so that it:

✓ Tells you how it feels

✓ Tells you what it thinks

✓ Tells you what it wants

✓ Tells you what it needs

This exercise will bring up some strong emotional issues that you may need to work through. This will help you gain insight and understanding of yourself and why you keep things.

You may also find that as you have released the subconscious issues that you no longer need that house and will let it go. I experienced this very clearly. I had bought an apartment in Melbourne that I absolutely loved. It looked down to the river and had lovely bay windows, it was in a beautiful heritage listed building.

One day I was looking at a cupboard and decided to move it to another spot. The minute I did that I KNEW I had finished with the apartment. So I went for a long walk, as you do, to have a coffee and think.

As I walked past a place I had loved before I bought my apartment but which had not been for sale then, I was astonished to see the real estate agent putting up a 'for sale' sign! I immediately asked for an inspection, made an offer and owned it 4 weeks later! I then rented out my other apartment.

I had bought my first unit after my marriage ended and while Mum was dying and looking back I realise that it was representing loss and sadness to me. Once I had released my grief I was able to sell it.

Within a few days of the sale I felt really good, as if the sunlight was switched on. I no longer felt sad when I thought of my mum but felt content with having had such a loving mother with me for so long. She was 95 when she died.

I would like to think that the apartment had done its job of nurturing me through those sad and difficult times and then eased me out at the right time! It helped me de-clutter my emotions!

If you have a long standing health or any other issue that hasn't resolved you might like to gain even more insight: do this exercise for every house/unit/flat you have ever lived in right from when you were born. When you compare the emotions you felt in each house you may find a very strong pattern develops which you need to clean out.

The important thing is to recognize why you are choosing the houses you choose and how much these houses satisfy your soul's needs.

VALUES AND AFFIRMATIONS

An affirmation is a positive statement that matches our feeling and has no resistance to it.

To make affirmations work for you it is best if you state the affirmation out loud and write it down at least 10 x per day until it is achieved.

Because we are working on Values a good affirmation is:

"Everything I am, everything I do, everything I say, everything I own reflects my true values"

As you do this affirmation every day listen to any ideas that may come to mind. These are clues to what your mind needs OR they are the resistances that you need to clear.

YOU WILL KNOW IF IT is a resistance by the way you *feel* when you say or write the affirmation. If it feels heavy, cloudy, sad, lonely, frustrated then it is resistance and you need to do the tapping exercise to neutralize it.

TAPPING EXERCISE 1

- Close your eye
- Tap the centre of the bone under your eyes with your index and middle fingers of both hands

Repeat this affirmation while tapping until your eyes open: 'Everything I *am* reflects my true values".

TAPPING EXERCISE 2

- Close your eyes
- Tap the centre of the bone under your eyes with your index and middle

fingers of both hands .

Repeat this affirmation while tapping until your eyes open "Everything I *do* reflects my true values".

TAPPING EXERCISE 3

- Close your eyes
- Tap the centre of the bone under your eyes with your index and middle fingers of both hands

Repeat this affirmation while tapping until your eyes open: 'Everything I *say* reflects my true values".

TAPPING EXERCISE 4

- Close your eyes
- Tap the centre of the bone under your eyes with your index and middle fingers of both hands

Repeat this affirmation while tapping until your eyes open: "Everything I *own* reflects my true values."

Often clients will say something along the lines of:

I was supposed to be a nurse like all the women in my family.

I was supposed to work a farm like dad does

I was supposed to do something special but I could never work out what that was

You know you are living up to others' expectations even if you love your work, are good at it, thrive at it but you always have a feeling that you are not doing what you are supposed to be doing.

This feeling that you are not doing what you are supposed to be doing may be because the ideas we receive from our family, friends or community *may not be right for us but they are part of u.s*

It is very enlightening to recognize the influence others have on our lives *often without us recognizing it.* Therefore this next exercise is a very valuable one for de-cluttering your mind.

You may think at first that no one has influenced you except you but many people find that when they explore this exercise further they discover otherwise. Some find that they have been passive aggressive by cluttering up the parent's home so they can 'get back at them'.

If you want to free yourself from restraints of what you're supposed to be doing so you can find out what you really want, you are going to have to find out *how* the messages came to you and *who* sent them.

EXERCISE TO RELEASE HIDDEN EXPECTATIONS

This next exercise is to be done in two ways so that all the hidden expectations are brought to the surface and explored.

Don't worry if you feel you are repeating yourself in some instances. It is better to repeat yourself than to miss someone.

In the table given below:

a) Write down your current work or career.

b) Working backwards write down every different type of work or career you have ever had over your lifetime.

c) In the next column write how old you were when you worked in that position.

d) In the next column write down the first name of any family member or significant person that comes to mind.

e) In the next column write down the feeling you felt when you identified that person.

f) In the next column write down what that person expected you to do.

Position Age/s Significant Person Feeling What they expected you to do

THE SECOND PART OF the exercise is similar.

In the table below:

a)Write down the name of everyone in your family and any significant others that you knew as you were growing up and as an adult.

This could be a relative, work colleague, a friend or even a public speaker or person whom you admired but had not yet met. Don't forget to include grandparents and brothers and sisters even if they are younger than you.

b) Next to that person's name write down what each person expected you to do. Do not judge what you write just put down the first thing that pops into your head

c) In the right hand column write down any feeling you had when you thought about what that person expected of you.

Person What they expected you to do Feeling

Once you have completed both of these exercises look at your tables and see if you can recognize a pattern within the expectations and feelings.

Perhaps you had nothing in the Expectations Column; perhaps there was a consistency in the expectations from significant females in your life or was there a consistency in the expectations from significant males in your life?

Once the patterns/feelings have been identified then it is time to let them go so you can have the right career that matches your life purpose and that makes you happy and healthy.

A strong *positive* feeling may mean that you chose that career in order to get your family member's approval just as a *negative* feeling may mean that you feel a failure because you did not fulfil their expectation of you.

It is certainly legitimate to want others to think well of us but many people live for the approval of others. Self-worth for them becomes based solely on how significant others view them. However the price of approval can become too high.

In reality you can only control your own happiness. If it is based on others' evaluations then even successes are transitory and enjoyed only briefly.

Living for approval is like feeding a never sated and ever hungry beast. If self -worth and happiness are based on the approval of others then you will never be happy in the long term.

There is a lovely story of an elderly couple. The wife always went to all the training and meditation classes she could throughout their years together; always lamenting that if only her husband went too he would learn so much and would become more spiritual.

One day her 'guru' decided to go to visit the husband who was pottering about in his garden. Here he met a man who was totally at peace with himself, his god and the world as he worked with the elementals and nature spirits achieving an harmonious place of beauty and peace. Everyone who walked past his garden was uplifted by the harmony of nature there. He was already at one with the universe and fulfilling his life purpose. There was nothing he needed to learn.

So often we forget that if we are doing what we love then we are living our life purpose. We do not have to achieve greatness or recognition or do what others think is meaningful work. We only have to be in harmony with ourselves to be in harmony with others and our life purpose.

A good affirmation is:

"Committed to living my life's purpose, I express my true self."

As you write this affirmation out 10 times (an ancient tradition of repeating something ten times to activate the Laws of Increase) listen to any ideas that may come to mind. These are clues to what your mind needs to be true to yourself or if they are negative they are the resistances you have to you being true to yourself.

You will know if it is a resistance by the way you feel when you say or write the affirmation. If it feels heavy, cloudy, sad, lonely, frustrated, then it is resistance and you need to do the tapping exercise to neutralize it.

TAPPING EXERCISE 1

- Close your eyes
- With your index and middle fingers of both hands tap the centre of the top of your head

While tapping repeat this statement until your eyes open "Even though I resist being committed to living my life's purpose, I accept myself completely and deeply".

TAPPING EXERCISE 2

- Close your eyes
- With your index and middle fingers of both hands tap the middle of the top of your head.

While tapping repeat this statement until your eyes open "Even though I resist expressing my true self, I accept myself completely and deeply "

Don't be surprised that as you do these tapping exercises you find yourself wanting to paint your house a different colour; wear different clothes; start to move things out of the house that you were quite comfortable having before. You are now starting to express your real self.

TAKE THE TIME TO VALUE YOURSELF

Mandela summed it up in his inaugural speech when he was elected president of South Africa.

"Our deepest fear is not that we are inadequate, our greatest fear is that we are powerful beyond measure.

It is our light not our darkness that most frightens us. We ask ourselves, who am I to be fabulous, brilliant, talented, gorgeous? Actually, who are you not to be, you are a child of God and your playing small does not serve the world. There is nothing enlightened about shrinking so that other people won't feel insecure around you. We are all meant to shine, like children do. We are born to manifest the glory of God within us. It is not just in some of us; it is in every one of us.

And as we let our own light shine, we unconsciously give people permission to do the same. As we are liberated by our fears, our presence automatically liberates others."

Is it so bad, then, to be misunderstood?

Pythagoras was misunderstood, and Socrates, and Jesus, and Luther, and Copernicus, and Galileo, and Newton, and every pure and wise spirit that ever took flesh. To be great is to be misunderstood."

A FINAL MESSAGE

So now you have completed reading through this book. Some very definite changes will have taken place *if* you have taken the time to do each of the exercises thoroughly and not just read them through.

PHOTOS

Remember I asked you to take a photo of yourself? Now it is important that you take another photo of yourself, your home, your car and compare them with the ones you took at the start of this book.

Look carefully, be honest and notice what changes have taken place both internally and externally. Notice what you notice. You may already have had friends tell you that they think that you are healthier, happier and younger looking and when you compare the photos you can now see clearly what they mean.

You will also notice changes around your house, your office, your car; in fact if you look closely you will see subtle and some not so subtle changes have occurred in your life.

Not only will you have de-cluttered your house but you notice that it doesn't get messy anymore; there is a special place for everything; that you put things away after you have used them rather than leaving them wherever you used them. You might now have a special hook near the door for your keys so you no longer have to hunt for them when you need to go out.

What is interesting is that often once we do the exercises in this book we do things that make our life easier without realising that we are doing them e.g. buying the key hook, knowing where everything is without having to hunt for items, we put things away so there is more space; the blinds and windows are open for fresh air.

Did you get that job or settlement you had been waiting a long time for? Did you paint the house?

Have you joined a new club/ taken up a new hobby? Are you exercising more? Do you feel fitter? Are you having more fun? All of these things indicate that you have released blockages to having a happier, healthier and more abundant life.

Now have a look at your life in general to clearly identify the changes that have occurred.

"If I had known I would live this long I would have taken better care of myself" – Eubie Blake on his 100th Birthday

What has changed? Is your home now easier to look after? Is it clean without having to go to huge effort?

Are you exercising more? How much more?

Are you eating organic vegetables?

Are you eating at home more and cooking your own food?

Have you bought/sold or are in the process of moving to a new house?

If so, what was the old house number? What is the new house number?

What do both these numbers represent?

Have you taken up a new sport? What is it?

Are you socially more active?

What are you doing specifically that you were not doing before ?

Have you met someone special?

WORK

Are you working for the same department at work or for the same organisation?

Has the work you are doing changed in any way?

Do you look forward to going to your work each day?

Sometimes a person will release one layer of emotions only to find that with time a deeper layer surfaces that needs to be cleared away. Revisiting the exercises contained within this book will help you remove these deeper layers.

I also like to apply Feng Shu principles to my home. It is certainly worth the cost to have a professional come to your home to assess it but only after you have de-cluttered. Otherwise the professional will spend your time and money telling you to throw out items to allow more energy into your home, to give clearer space and aesthetics.

THANK YOU FOR PURCHASING my book. I hope you found the exercises useful, you have a fresh new home and outlook on life and I look forward to working with you again.

IF YOU WOULD LIKE TO find out more or do some more exercises to help you to live the life you want, please see my *"Free to be Healthy" and "Free to be Healthy Workbook"* also on Kindle, print on demand and at my website www.mangotiger.com.au[1]

AUTHOR AND CONSULTANT

For over 43 years Margaret Cutler has worked with clients throughout the world helping them to identify and release the thoughts, beliefs and emotions that were negatively affecting their health and lives in general.

In 1997 she was Nominated Citizen of Australia for her work with the subconscious mind.

Margaret has been continually listed in Who's Who of Australian Writers since 1986. Her educational books are for students of all ages including" How to Understand Poetry" and "How to Write Essays, Short Stories, Novels, Reports and Summaries" which is recognized for its outstanding and unique technique to make writing easy. These books are on Kindle as eBooks and print on demand as well as in most universities, schools and general libraries throughout Australia.

Please contact Margaret through her website www.mangotiger.com.au[2] if you would like her help, for her to speak at any of your groups or to run a workshop.

---

1. http://www.mangotiger.com.au

2. http://www.mangotiger.com.au

Don't miss out!

Visit the website below and you can sign up to receive emails whenever Margaret Cutler publishes a new book. There's no charge and no obligation.

https://books2read.com/r/B-A-JNABB-NQLPC

BOOKS 2 READ

Connecting independent readers to independent writers.

About the Author

Nominated Citizen of Australia for her work with the subconscious Mind Margaret has been listed in Who's who of Australian Authors since 1986.

Combining case studies, exercises and techniques Margaret takes you on a fascinating journey into your subcosncius mind to find the hidden thoughts, beliefs and emotions that are holding you back from having the life you want.

Read more at https://www.mangotiger.com.au.

www.ingramcontent.com/pod-product-compliance
Lightning Source LLC
Chambersburg PA
CBHW050602160726
48003CB00003B/1009